Wild Song

CARD

Wild Song

Poems *of the* Natural World

EDITED BY JOHN DANIEL

Illustrations by Deborah Randolph Wildman

The University of Georgia Press   *Athens & London*

©1998 by the University of Georgia Press
Athens, Georgia 30602
Illustrations © by Deborah Randolph Wildman
All rights reserved
Designed by Sandra Strother Hudson

Printed digitally in the United States of America

Library of Congress Cataloging-in-Publication Data
Wild song : poems of the natural world / edited by John Daniel ;
illustrations by Deborah Randolph Wildman.
xii, 129 p. : ill. ; 22 cm.
ISBN 0-8203-2011-0 (pbk : alk. paper)
1. Nature—Poetry. 2. American poetry—20th century.
I. Daniel, John, 1948– .
PS595.N22W55 1998
811'.5'08036—dc21   97-49514

British Library Cataloging-in-Publication Data available

Most of the poems appeared previously in *Wilderness*
magazine, published by the Wilderness Society,
and are used here by permission.

Contents

PART TWO

PART THREE

PART FOUR

PART FIVE

Preface

Early in 1988 I wrote Tom Watkins, editor of *Wilderness*, urging him to publish poetry in the magazine. To my surprise, and perhaps to his, Tom wrote back, "Why don't we give it a shot? You're the poetry editor."

We were willing to bet that the membership of the Wilderness Society, cultivated by a long tradition of literary prose, would appreciate good poems of the natural world. By 1990 the Wildsong page had become one of the most popular features of the magazine. Many readers wrote to say that they read the poems before anything else. I was receiving three to four thousand poems a year, from every state, several Canadian provinces, and a few countries of Europe.

Tom and other environmental editors have long known that their publications must do more than convey information. Readers are exposed to swarms of facts, most of them dismal; readers *respond* to grace and power of language, the emotional resonance it evokes. Poetry, with its rhythmic intensities, its rich directions and indirections of meaning, can ignite small explosions of clarity. "It's not just something for scholars to write about," Adrienne Rich has said. "It's a way in which people can hear their own unspoken thoughts spoken."

Over the years I tried to welcome to the Wildsong page a wide variety of North American creatures, weathers, and landscapes. I didn't limit the forum to poems about wilderness in a strict sense. I looked for poems touching or touched by wild nature, poems that show us the wilderness within and around us all the time.

In order to include many voices in our limited space, I tilted toward short poems in a variety of forms. I solicited work from most of the prominent poets I admire; at the same time, I tried to reserve at least half the page for poets unknown or little known nationally.

This book collects some of the verse published or accepted for publication in *Wilderness* from 1988 to 1997—celebrations, laments, tales, meditations, mysteries great and small. A current sampler of the spoken wild. I hope you enjoy it.

JOHN DANIEL
Winter Creek, Oregon

One

Seasonal

The man who burst into leaf
in springtime sprouted
delicate twigs from his scalp.
Green buds unfurled on his cheeks
where a beard had once flourished
and on the backs of his hands
instead of fine hairs. They thought
that they would never see
a grown man behaving
like a tree, his friends avowed
and predicted that before long
he would fall into the sere
and yellow leaf. Some suggested
pruning on the chance he'd bear
more fruit. Neighborhood children
came to swing from his limbs,
and birds sang in his upper branches.
They dropped something on his head.
When he swayed on the lawn
in a high wind, his wife accused him
of being drunk again.
His heartbeat slowed. He began
to listen to the weather.

John Nixon Jr.

Sassafras

Here, straight
From inarticulate
Sod, it arises,
Tartly surprises
With a swift eloquence
Sharper than mint's.
Those who, alas,
Do not speak sassafras
Are urged to taste one verb,
Crush a superb
Phrase in the mouth. It bites
The taster. It recites.

Jody Gladding

Artichoke

Summer's yield
will be apparent, offered
up from vine or down from bent
stem. But now, I need
to get on my hands and knees
to dig the leeks out by their roots,
to pry open the clenched ferns
and snap off their curled digits
before they grow straight
and poisonous, to pull the bitter
dandelion greens and spikes of chive
out from between grass blades.
I need to wait down there
for the crimped rhubarb leaf to let
out stalk, which isn't poisonous,
only so stringy, so tart,
who'd ever think of sucking on it?
This craving's more
than hunger. Winter's left me
miserly, lying in my root cellar,
dull-eyed and spineless.
Give me the thistle bud,
boiled in vinegar. Let me hold
each petal by its claw and scrape
them through my teeth. Let me clean
the needles from the bile-green
heart, quarter it,
and eat each chamber whole.

Malcolm Glass

Little Sonnet for Spring

Cold in clouds, the sun sent scant
light glancing along the ridge. Fog
rose from the stream, a descant
in a minor key, an analogue

glossing the major mode of song
played by distant mountains, a plaid
of greens, not one patch or hue wrong.
It was as though the landscape had

always been muted, perfect, so
contained. On other days the sun
sharpens the spines of the leaves, blows
ragged the edges of the hills.

Today dull overcast blurred sky
and soil in whispers for the eye.

Mary Gray

When I Am Wise

When I am wise in the speech of grass,
I forget the sound of words
and walk into the bottomland
and lie with my head on the ground
and listen to what grass tells me
about small places for wind to sing,
about the labor of insects,
about shadows dank with spice,
and the friendliness of weeds.

When I am wise in the dance of grass,
I forget my name and run
into the rippling bottomland
and lean against the silence which flows
out of the crumpled mountains
and rises through slick blades, pods,
wheat stems, and curly shoots,
and is carried by wind for miles
from my outstretched hands.

Wendell Berry

The Best Reward

(from *Sabbaths*)

The best reward in going to the woods
Is being lost to other people, and
Lost sometimes to myself. I'm at the end
Of no bespeaking wire to spoil my goods;

I send no letter back I do not bring.
Whoever wants me now must hunt me down
Like something wild, and wild is anything
Beyond the reach of purpose not its own.

Wild is anything that's not at home
In something else's place. This good white oak
Is not an orchard tree, is unbespoke,
And it can live here by its will alone,

Lost to all other wills but Heaven's—wild.
So where I most am found I'm lost to you,
Presuming friend, and only can be called
Or answered by a certain one, or two.

Thomas R. Smith

In Late Winter

The frozen lake never loses its patience
with winter. On an appointed day in April
the loon will meet its reflection in open water.

Imagination opens again to earth. We
believe in bees, the wild rose's grail filled
with summer. The watery twin comes nearer.

Letha Elliott

Vermont Spring

Walking in spring
never far from the sound
of rushing water,
I came to a clearing
in the woods.
A silver birch stood
with me, silent.

A woodpecker beat time,
momentarily,
with my pounding heart,
and, in a marshy pond,
swollen with liquid snows,
something small, unseen,
broke the surface
to breathe the air.

Back in the brittle city,
where voices and corners
are sharp,
the surfaces concrete-hard—
important—
and silence is a memory,
something small, unseen
within me
breaks the surface
to breathe the wooded air.

Parliament of Fowls on Dog River

I had not thought so many birds around—
Then from behind the red-camellia bush
The hid night-heron rose with raucous "grokk!"
And whurry of wings, breaking the twilight hush.
Just seconds later, after the sudden shock,
Countless birds exploded into sound.
They all berated him: the sputtering thrush,
The spitting cardinal, the screaming jay,
The shrieking mockingbird—each had his say,
Loud and most indignant, with curses round
And scorching hot. I never knew before
That any birds save parrots ever swore.
Such frightful expletives I'd never heard
From any human, much less from a bird!
But yelled that furious Parliament of Fowls:
"Fry that heron's entrails! Boil his bowels!
Break his beak! Tan his hide for leather!
Slit his tongue! Pluck out every feather!
Grind up his gizard, kidneys, brains, and liver
And feed them to the 'gators in the river!
May turtles gobble up his rotten heart!
Of all his eggs may there survive ne'er 'un!
Curses! curses! on that black night-heron!"

That's what they said. Or something of the sort.

The heron didn't stay, but thought it best
To fly up-river and rob some other nest.

The Ferns

They unwind in darkness
like a dream
of freedom
passing between fugitives
in love.
The day, now and then,
peers down,
catching their movements;
but the ferns,
vigilant as owls,
quiet their spiralling breath
and disguise
each passionate unfolding
behind mild, green,
impassive bows.

Ingrid Wendt

The Thing to Do

Though what I did that day was right,
reporting the rattlesnakes coiled tightly
together—diamond-backed lovers
oblivious to my step within a breath of
leaves crackling under the bush;

though he did what he had to,
hacking them dead with his long-handled
garden hoe, flinging the still-
convulsing whips of their passion into
the bed of his pickup—that scene,

bright vulture of memory, stays;
picks this conscience that won't
come clean: this wasn't
the way the story would go
those times I wondered if ever

I'd see my own rattlesnake out in the wild,
having listened through years of summer
hikes, in the likeliest places, without
once hearing that glittering warning
said to be unmistakable; knowing

since childhood, the thing to do is not
flicker a muscle, to stare the face of danger
down as though it didn't exist.
No rattlesnake ever had eyes for another.
And menace never multiplied, one season to next.

Where a Deer Fell

my daughter uncovers bones,
overgrown with briar, glued to soil
by leafmeal and frost.
The forest floor clings as
we lift the skull into light, examining the
little spirit that remains,
the brittle nostrils opened to wind, the eyes filled
with the darkness of small ponds.

Shoots of honeysuckle, green briar and grape,
a tendril of ivy and finger of mandrake
push through the spinal canal, separate
vertebrae, disjoin knee from shank and hip from thigh,
encircle a bleached jaw, tie the toothy
mandible like stone to earth, lacing the caved ribs
with vine, pulling the whitened bones back
into more ancient flesh.

Arches

When you come here, if you can,
See yourself in these rocks full of sky.
They are no more weathered than
Your mind. In you as well a high
Desert cliff extrudes a span.
In you as well a constant dry
Wind proceeds without a plan.
In you as well there petrify
Spaces you were going to expand,
Springs you were about to start from
Into an expanse of sand,
Gestures you can never part from.

John Daniel

Spring Burning

One April morning in the rain I pile green boughs
from the big Douglas fir
whose limbs had sagged on the barn,
splash gas, toss a match, and *whump*
out of nowhere, an orange explosion
subsiding to a hesitant burn,
flames stirring like sleepy children
still thralled by the other world,
then a quickening hiss and crackle
of sap-gorged wood, and the flames
remember their yellow hunger,
climbing the heaped greens with a rising roar.
I heave more branches,
my hat lowered to the sheer smack of heat
that instantly sizzles the needle-sprays black,
singes my mustache, curls
the hairs on the backs of my hands,
and I wonder as I carry
big sections of limb
I had planned to season for stovewood,
how we ever got it locked in the tips of matches
or in motors purring at our feet,
how we trained it to simmer saucepans
and stand, docile, on candle wicks,
a flutter as one of us walks by
the one slight sign
that once the world was its blasting cauldron

and is that now, within.
Live, I say, tossing scrap wood now,
rotted shingles and posts,
a wobbly sawhorse, plywood pieces—
live now, and not this summer.
But it isn't for prudence or good housekeeping
that I feed and feed
that unbearable aura,
it's for the flames that exult around each gift,
transmuting hard heft
in their red livid heart
to the nothing it actually is.
Ashes drift down with the sprinkling rain.
With no more to offer
I stand aside, gazing like a child
at the great burning tent I will someday enter—
it gathers itself
from the dull clay ground,
it writhes and yearns, it points
to the far, invisible stars it has not forgotten.

Don Colburn

Morning Song

Day breaks open artlessly
across a field of switchgrass tossing
wild and easy in the windswell.
The weedy fastness gives way to a widening
brim of eastlight blazing the mist.
Spring is the dangerous season, awakening
this bee-crazed meadow to overgrowing—
and in me awe, and ache, avid to begin
like birds and the earth all over.

Marc Harshman

Byng Inlet, Ontario

Sun-whitened rocks
mottled with rust and silver lichens
slant unbroken and still
into the rolling bay.
The water burns
its purple tide against the land.
Birch and spruce twist south and east
away from the north, the imprint of winter
stiff in them where they mount
isolated and ragged their flags
on the sloping headlands.
It is spring in the North.
We are allowed now.
Sandpipers skitter the stony shores.
The heron glides in awkward grace.
The wolf and marten retreat
toward shadows, snow, that safety
north of understanding.

Pattiann Rogers

In My Time

It's easy to praise things present—the belligerent
stance of the woodhouse toad, the total
self-absorption of the frostweed blossom.
It's simple to compliment a familiar mess
of curly dock, the serene organization
of common onion reeds, the radish bulb
and its slender purple tail. And I like the way
the jay flings dirt furiously this morning
from the window box, the ridiculous shakings
of his black beak.

But it's not easy to praise things yet-to-come—
the nonexistent nubs of mountains not risen
from beneath the floor of the sea
or a new sound from some new creature,
descended maybe from our golden peepers
and white-chinned chuggers, that sound
becoming synonomous, for someone else,
with spring.

How can I appreciate light from an aging
sun shining through new configurations neither pine
nor ash? How can I extol the nurturing
fragrances from the spires, the spicules
of a landscape not yet formed or seeded?

I can praise these flowers today—the white yucca
with its simmering powder-covered moth, the desert
tahoka daisy and the buffalo gourd—but never
the future strangeness that may eventually
take their places.

From here now, I simply praise in advance
the one who will be there then,
so moved, as I, to do the praising.

Two

Work

This is the house
that must be entered,
the house whose doors
do not lock,
whose walls are shadow
of moving trees,

the house whose table
is heavy with food
already blessed,
waiting under
the mouths in need
of food, of blessing,

the house whose windows
were polished until
they vanished,
whose moon and sun
once painted there
moved inside,

the one whose chimney
breathes a visible
breath at night,
the house whose walls
must be swept
with the wing of a bird.

Teacher

Stillness and silence deepen with the last light.

Across the glossy luminous water a muskrat
noses a passage, trailing a clean wake.
Nearer, circles ripple outward where a fish
came up with open jaws on a mayfly.

The fire crumbles down, crackling.
Near the canoe, the washed skillet and plates
drip upside down onto a cold rock-shelf.

The wind begins to breathe and blow
through the spruce-tops, they creak and the food duffle
sways where we hung it, up in the branches, high.

At this little lake, this floor
of one shaft of heaven, the peppermint
we trampled when we were hammering stakes
scents our darkness inside the tent;
mosquitoes patter against the nylon like rain.

We shift and settle our hips and shoulders
till they'll accept their own weight. It's only
a little, what we know or hope to know.
The loons seem to break their laughter with a cry.

Simple Mysteries

Lupine, for example: its dry
Mediterranean clinging to the hills, its gray-green
furry pods, its beaked flowers like
a woman's genitals—the wide banners and small wings
and the closed, smooth keel—the love of bees
for it, the private smell of lupine flesh, the fishlike
glimmer of its yellow heart, the deep blue
blossoms strung on stems above
the blue-gray palmate leaves
like flocks of small, intensely colored birds
blurring the hillsides into fields of blue, the world
broken into flower
without our even asking.

Naomi Shihab Nye

Fireflies

Lately I had looked for you everywhere
but only night's smooth stare gazed back.

Some said DDT had cupped your glow
in its sharp mouth and swallowed.
The loneliness of growing up
held small soft pockets you could have filled.

This summer I carried my son
to the Texas hills where you startled us at dark,
ancestral droves swirling about our heads.
He thought you carried kerosene lamps
the size of splinters. He wanted to borrow one,
just for a second, he said.
My head swooned in the blink of your lives.

Near a cedar-shaded stream where by day
fish rise for crumbled lumps of bread,
you were saving us from futures bereft
of minor lovely things.
You're singing, my boy said that night.
Why are you singing? He opened his hands.
I sang to the quiet rise of joy,
to little light.

Deborah A. Miranda

Echolocation

For the bats at the Point Defiance Zoo

All day long you flutter through artificial night;
hover, sway, wrap furred bodies in leathery shawls
after aborted flight, cling to false stalactites.
Do you know when the moon outside is full,
do you miss the veering, all-out beats
of easy strength across the lunar face,
every stroke of wingspan a simple masterpiece?
Do you remember the soaring, twirling, swooping pace,
the snap of insects' hard chitinous shells,
soft velvet of a moth's frantic wings?
You eat, excrete, mate, bear young in your tiny cell
but does a warm summer night's calling
echo like a long jagged cave twisting deep into stone,
reverberate against your blood and bone?

Leonard Nathan

Sequoia

In the middle of the ancient woods
leaves browse on the sun like gods,
roots tongue the dark below—
who needs words? I find myself
debating silence, and losing again.

Wendell Berry

The Vacation

Once there was a man who filmed his vacation.
He went flying down the river in his boat
with his video camera to his eye, making
a moving picture of the moving river
upon which his sleek boat moved swiftly
toward the end of his vacation. He showed
his vacation to his camera, which pictured it,
preserving it forever: the river, the trees,
the sky, the light, the bow of his rushing boat
behind which he stood with his camera
preserving his vacation even as he was having it
so that after he had had it he would still
have it. It would be there. With a flick
of a switch, there it would be. But he
would not be in it. He would never be in it.

Jonathan Till

Recording an Archaeological Site for the San Juan County Sanitary Landfill

Between two arms
of outcropping mudstone
in a small gully that trails out
into baked clay flats of
hardy shadscale and snakeweed.

The mudstone rocks are black
with a sheen beat into them
by this solstice sun.
Hot air ripples, burns eyes,
bends my gaze down to a point.

To a point!

The blade is perfect,
flake scars delicate
and precise with patience,
knapped from a creamy gray chert.

And what of our traces left here
for future eyes in a thousand years?
Broken plastic knives,
brown beer bottle glass,

a tarnished coin that fell
amongst black rocks.

William Johnson

Black Lead Mountain

Where the trail climbs free of brush
and the bony trunks of whitebarks
we watch it rise, a blunt thumb
brooding over the valley,
the place last summer
scarred by fire, where a boy
was never found. Today white rags
skim the nape of its peak
and my son is amazed how far
he can squint through haze
to the Bitterroots, jagged,
worn teeth clamped in a jaw. For days
Black Lead Mountain surrounds us.
We camp and fish in its shadow,
wake to a shroud of mist
where the moon has fallen.
The gnarled trunk where my son
has propped his pack leans
like a twisted crone,
its roots acknowledging ice
and a slow indigenous burning
in the mountain's shadow,
always, only the earth.

T. K. André-Eames

Under the Sun

A dying snake gleams upright in the sun,
his ribbon stiffened just where he would wriggle,
his curving water patched into dry sunlight.
The small intense suns that were his eyes
slow to twin moons of muted brightness.
Slipping away, his life drifts in the orbs
that lift above. His long skin is still.
What darkness sucks the ripple from his bones,
this lonely filament, so odd and small?
What darkness makes such oddness of us all?

Jane Hirshfield

For a Wedding on Mount Tamalpais

July,
and the rich apples
once again falling.

You put them to your lips,
as you were meant to,
enter a sweetness
the earth wants to give.

Everything loves this way,
in gold honey,
in gold mountain grass
that carries lightly the shadow of hawks,
the shadow of clouds passing by.

And the dry grasses,
the live oaks and bays,
taste the apples' deep sweetness
because you taste it, as you were meant to,
tasting the life that is yours,

while below, the fog horns bend to their work,
bringing home what is coming home,
blessing what goes.

Ronald F. Smits

Wetlands

Let me legislate for wetlands
within our bodies—back bays, swamps,
mossy ravines, underground streams,
rapids that we ride for pleasure.

Joseph Powell

Camping in the Cascades

Hungry for bootprints, shades of differences,
we've come to think like the earth.
In the valley below, it was summer,
dim air-conditioned houses sulked,
days flat as fallow fields.
We climb back in time:
yellow fawn lillies, shooting stars,
ferns curled tight as snails.

We meet grimed climbers coming down,
each wrapped in a heavy calm
that bears the unsteady weight of each foot.
Out of the blue, one mountain
after another steps forward, beckoning.
How far can we go?
Finally, at Deep Lake, other tents
scattered along the shore,
we eat and watch a half-moon rise.
The stars that guided seafarers,
kings, whole milleniums of geese,
awaken slowly in the uninterrupted sky.

Our lives shrink to incandescent flames
that blink on the surface of the lake.
Smoke climbs its rope of air
and disappears into the dark

like our own best thoughts.
Nocturnal eyes open, claws flex.
Faithfully, we lie on the ground
spinning slowly through space.
Heavenly bodies shine through our sleep.

C. L. Rawlins

The River

Maybe what I'll do:
walk down to the river,
walk down on the trail
where sand loves my feet
and wants to keep them.

Maybe I'll walk down, slow
as these red-and-black ants
when the long shadow covers us,
alone and cool on the trail,
looking around, half dreaming,
through cottonwoods with lamb's ear leaves,
seeing how tamarisk and russian olive
chase coyote willow from the floodplain,
meandering among the thorns.

Maybe these thin lines of blood
incised by my direction
are tributaries to the whole notion
of going on: the necessary river
red and gold with earth, here
and gone through sandstone canyons
into the low sun as clouds return
full and flush with watered light,
bound for headwaters.

Maybe I'll get there soon,
drop my shoes and leave
a whorled print in slick silt
next to a raccoon track;
step down in and stand there looking
as muddy, cool mountain water
parts around my skin;

maybe this is how it is:
maybe this is how it is.

San Juan River, Utah

Ronald Wallace

Pileated

It's much too big for words,
this Woody Woodpecker of a bird,
this cartoon creature
all wires and pulleys, that slams
into the old dead elm and,
for a moment, rejuvenates it:
a flicker of fire, a flare
on the gray, decaying bark.

And before we can even say *it's a,*
it's a, a . . . it's gone,
this remnant, this
premise, taking
the sky, the light, the summer,
our blue eyes with it.

William Stafford

Walking at the Beach

Inside the ocean flow great rivers
never discovered, known only to themselves,
Amazons without any shore. And as we
walk I feel those currents. Lilting,
flickering clouds of sandpipers whisk by.
Gulls pose their silhouettes—heavy at both
ends when they walk—along the sand. A faint
gray ship ghosts the horizon. Ocean air
presses its fingers through our sweaters
and streams on, shaking the beach grass.
Our friends the slanted old spruce trees darken
all the headlands, leaning away from the sea
but watching over their shoulders. Out there
somewhere in that welter and flow a great seething
story unites us, passing with a majesty so tall
that its glance almost makes us disappear.

Andrés Rodríguez

The Earth

She scooped a handful of shiny pebbles
   from the riverbed, held them
   a long time to her face,
a morning of clear light all around us.

The river stopped, the far hills glowed,
   and from where we knelt
   on the gritty bank
the soft summer air moved on us.

She took care for the smallest things:
   remembering to touch
   the unmoved stones, to breathe
with her body the whole expanse of light.

All day I dreamed the earth was rising
   from bedrock, from alluvium,
to the wind's slow motion,
   a dance taking ages to perform.

Three

Bruce Berger

Visitation

I stargazed from my bedroll.
Out of perfect quiet
A rush of living dark
Tore through the Milky Way
With muffled wings, a great
Shadow wheeled and paused
Over my heart, then dropped
Earthward till the shriek
Of no pale rabbit broke
My breath. The startled owl
Slid from our shared panic
And left to silence the icy
Scrawl of our galaxy.

Maxine Kumin

Down East News Item

In a stove-in fifties Cadillac
crashed in a quarry west of Brunswick
two bear cubs and their matriarch
have taken up abode. The sow
dozes behind the wheel, the cubs
bask against the windshield. How
they got down there, most likely crab-
wise, scuttling when they dared
from shelf to shelf, we'll never know.

Since feckless humans hurl their garbage
down the rock face to be spared
composting it (though you might say
it gets composted either way
in time) the bears don't need to forage.
Here comes the satisfying splat
of rotted squash, the ratatat
of chicken bones, the tick of pans
still stickered with takeout dividends,
manna that raises a tatted crust
on fenders roseate with rust.

A dazzle of August sunlight sleeks
the tail fins into almost-motion
but later, when cold darkness licks
rime-deep into their twisted bastion

the sow will claw a ragged cave
in the upholstery stuffing
and maybe they'll all three survive
into another kingdom come.
Elsewhere General Motors hums.

Mary Oliver

Opossum

The dogs descend,
prancing and loping, ready to brawl, but it
lies down at their approach, and plays
dead,

and so I have
a good look, in the starlight,
at the monkey tail, and the stumped lightning of the teeth,
and the spidery hands,

and the eyes which
won't focus, won't
look at me. It is
a small pig with a savage head—

a bloated flute, lying
in the wet grass.
I call the dogs away
and I think very soon they forget—

but all day I imagine
how it got up, finally, when we were gone,
and sighed, and shook itself—
how it minced away

down the old ditches—how it scurried
through the damp leaves, to some pleated
circlet of slumped oak.
All day the dogs

are gone on their rounds of adventures—
and as for myself—at any cost
it is the present I lay claim to—
it is the dangerous and marvelous future

I mean to find.
And yet, how it stays in my mind—
a little landslide of perfect responses—
a gray baby ghost,

its pale snout turning,
its five-fingered spider hands tapping,
in drowsy circles,
the mossy banks of the past.

Another Little God

You don't know how important
it might be—the blue-white light
from a star like Vega caught in the eyedots
of nocturnal grass frogs and yellow-bellied
toads, caught in the senses of fishing
bats, mouse-tailed bats.

And I can't say either how much
it might matter—that same ping
of light multiplied by each reflective
grain of crystal sand along a beach
beside the Gulf, held by each slide
and scissor of beak rushes
in a southern marsh.

Maybe particles and shafts of light
from Vega penetrate the earth, descend
through silt and loam, touching,
even enlivening, even partially defining
the microscopic roots of bellflowers,
purple vetches and peas, the creases
and shackles of worm snakes and grubs.

The translucent eggs of the plumed moth,
the fins of the redbelly dace might *need*
a star's blue-white light, like water,
like air. Breath might require it,

breathing starlight into the heart.
You don't know. After all, we've never
lived without it.

If starlight spears through each oily
sperm link of reedbuck and potto,
if it enters every least bulb
of snow flea, wheel bug, hay
louse, if it corridors through all bone
crystals, around each spurl and bole
of the brain, inside timbre and voice,
piercing the whole stone and space
of *believe*, then, if only for one
complete name under the sky tonight,
lie still and remember.

Wendell Berry

The Lowland Grove

(from *Sabbaths*)

And now the lowland grove is down, the trees
Fallen that had unearthly power to please
The earthly eye, and gave unearthly solace
To minds grown quiet in that quiet place.
To see them standing was to know a prayer
Prayed to the Holy Spirit in the air
By that same Spirit dwelling in the ground.
The wind in their high branches gave the sound
Of air replying to that prayer. The rayed
Imperial light sang in the leaves it made.

To live as mourner of a human friend
Is but to understand the common end
Told by the steady counting in the wrist.
For though the absent friend is mourned and missed
At every pulse, it is a human loss
In human time made well; our grief will bless
At last the dear lost flesh and breath; it will
Grow quiet as the body in the hill.

To live to mourn an ancient woodland, known
Always, loved with an old love handed down,
That is a grief that will outlast the griever,
Grief as landmark, grief as a wearing river
That in its passing stays, biding in rhyme
Of year with year, time with returning time,

As though beyond the grave the soul will wait,
In long unrest, the shaping of the light
In branch and bole, through centuries that prepare
This ground to pray again its finest prayer.

John Quinn

Mojave Coontail

A muscular buzz in the creosote brush—
　　sound as thick as your forearm
　　flexes through the desert dusk:

The preacher with the tambourine tail
　　rides his dusty, twilight circuit,
　　taking the word to rabbit and quail:

Diamonds and stripes in a pastel light—
　　no gospel ever traveled so well,
　　no scripture ever seemed so right:

Toward us he seems quite circumspect
　　veering from his chosen text
　　though still in serpent dialect:

Gather your children; gather your wives;
　　leave this desert to me and mine;
　　go home to your own troubled lives.

Alison Hawthorne Deming

Sanctuary

(from *The Monarchs*)

In Mexico where the eastern monarchs
gather for their winter sleep,
a tide of fluttering orange and black
sweeping over the border and into the trees
of the central mountains, there is
such hunger that the campesinos,
though their fathers and mothers
believe the butterflies are
spirits of the dead returning,
must cut the forest for fuel and cropland.
Brush smoking, burned pits of stumps,
scrawny pony, burro tethered in the cut corn,
footpaths worn in the lower woods.
In the sanctuary, the lofty remains of the cloud forest,
vigilantes guide the pilgrims under the dark canopy
of ancient trees and into the wind of butterfly wings.
In the heat of the afternoon
the monarchs come down from their sleep
to huddle on the edges of streams and
meadow pools, trembling to stay warm,
and they sip, then sit, then fly off
until the air is a blizzard of orange.
The pilgrims watch quietly, lines of
school children from Mexico City,
scientists from Texas, Florida, California,
old women in rebozos on the arms

of their adult sons, tourists with
cameras and binoculars. And together
they drink in the spectacle
with the great thirst they have brought
from their cities and towns, and it is
a kind of prayer, this meeting of our kind,
so uncertain how to be
the creature we are, and theirs,
so clear in their direction.

A Second Before It Bursts

Seeing my reflection on a river
   and seeing a bubble float into my reflection
      the bubble also reflecting me,
So I see the reflection of my face in a bubble
   in the reflection of my face
      on the river,
While below on the bottom
   the shadow of the bubble passes over
      golden fallen sunken leaves
So it looks like inside my face is a riverbottom
   of golden fallen sunken leaves
      with the shadow of a bubble passing over
   while on the surface
My reflected face with a bubble moving in it
   also reflecting me
      and me thinking
It will burst any second
   just before it
      bursts. . . .

Robert Bly

A Private Fall

Motes of haydust rise and fall
with slow and grave steps,
like servants who dance in the yard
because some prince has been born.

What has been born? The winter.
Then the Egyptians were right.
Everything wants a chance to die,
to begin in the clear fall air.

Each leaf sinks and goes down
when we least expect it.
We glance toward the window for some
thing has caught our eye.

It's possible autumn is a tomb
out of which a child is born.
We feel a secret joy
and we tell no one!

William Stafford

A Slant Message

Tell them how tame geese lure wild ones
close, and then what happens. Go ahead,
explain. Give all the usual reasons
that people use for their treachery.

Far off, mingled with wind and rain, coasting
their strong wings clearly down a long
staircase of air, the wild ones turn arcs
of trust, mated for life by their truth.

Sometimes I wake, my wings are set, dawn
has targeted my face, I hear voices
calling me in. My steep dive true
into the world ends my wide dream.

Faint all day in the sky, trails thrill
their way, like this, into my talk, my telling.

Chainsaw

The way it pops and razzes
and grumbles under its breath,
the way it hefts in your grip
then shrieks lickety-split
through the thick log, leaving
the burnt arc in the bit
of log left, the way
it fills the woods
with its angular whang,
smoke drifted like dust
from a battle, the way
it conjures its rage and goes
into whatever lies in its way
makes you wonder often
if it aims to turn on you
like a serpent, or some force
hurled up from underground.
Why else would it bare
its shiny silver teeth and smile,
ready to leap in your hand?

Reg Saner

The Raven

Where summer's best effort is tufts
slate-green or ashen, a caw flapping off stone
came boulder to boulder toward me
floating low over tundra.

If its "Qua! . . . Qua! . . ." echoed
inside me as Latin, what perched by my lunch
weren't wings out of books,
just local and raven. With a beak scuffed up
from grubbing its life out of faces
patient as granite, it peppered my flicks
of canned tuna, my bread bits, my cashews.
Then stared. As if I were empty.

Down over Arapahoe Pass
November chill rolled by us as vapor
till the only motion not mine was old
if not ancient, a raven into whose eye
other hikers had come, and cloudbanks
into which they had gone.

Jane Hirshfield

On the Beach

Uncountable tiny pebbles
of many colors.

Broken seashells mixed in with whole ones.

Sand dollars, shattered and whole,
the half-gone wing of a gull.

Changed glass
that is like the heart after much pain.
The empty shell of a crab.

A child moves alone in the gray
that is half fog, half wind-blown ocean.

She lifts one pebble, another,
into her pocket.
From time to time takes them out again and looks.

These few and only these. How many? Why?

The waves continue their work of breaking
then rounding the edges.

I would speak to her if I could,
but across the distance what would she hear?
Ocean and ocean. Cry of a fish.

—Walk slowly now, small soul, by the edge
of the water. Choose carefully
all you are going to lose, though any of it would do.

Mary Gray

The Shadow of My Hand

When the sun rolls up, orange,
over the bay, and I lift my hand and cup it
to shield my eyes, and its shadow slides
off my knee and falls into the marsh reeds,
and finds its own kind waiting there
among the mumbling ducks and waves,
it's my hand that's let it go, after all—
my hand which on cloudy days keeps its shadow
locked in, invisible, as if it doesn't exist,
though of course it always does,
or my hand couldn't, either,
floating above its shadow on sunny days,
as a heron lays its image on the bay.
And at night, stars burning, moon high,
when I walk the lanes of salt grass
to stand beneath the old cypress,
whose branches reach into the world
with bold twists, whose roots clasp
minuscule secrets of dirt and rocks,
the shadow of my hand is first to touch
the twining sinews of bark my hand so loves.

The Grand Canyon

As if there were instead some limit
To this world which follows where we go;
As if we could renounce the many
Habits we acquired long ago;
As if we could embrace the infinite
Spaces we traverse like falling snow;
Or as if we ourselves had any
Substance, and were present; even so,
Just when we are ready to admit
Defeat we find ourselves on this plateau
Staring out across long violet
Reaches filling up with indigo.

Four

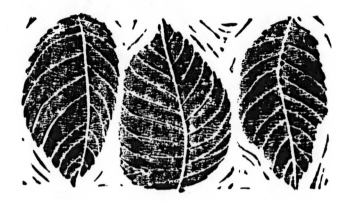

Denise Levertov

Open Secret

Perhaps one day I shall let myself
approach the mountain—
hear the streams which must flow down it,
lie in a flowering meadow, even
touch my hand to the snow.
Perhaps not. I have no longing to do so.
I have visited other mountain heights.
This one is not, I think, to be known
by close scutiny, by touch of foot or hand
or entire outstretched body; not by any
familiarity of behavior, any acquaintance
with its geology or the scarring roads
humans have carved in its flanks.
This mountain's power
lies in the open secret of its remote
apparition, silvery low-relief
coming and going moonlike at the horizon,
always loftier, lonelier, than I ever remember.

Cygnus

Long past sunset while I split green wood
the trumpeter swan left our shallow lake.
We had not seen its mate all summer.
Four times it circled overhead before
turning toward a darkening mountain pass.
A man at Trapper Creek once told me
old-timers called them swamp-turkeys.
It was late October and he wore
a hat made from the head of a wolf.
I watched that swan until it disappeared.
Now the absence of its beating wings
sounds a sadness nesting in my heart:
soon only that far constellation will
recall what was once so wonderful and wild.

Kathryn Winograd

Garden Snake

Yes, I know the garden.
And the autumn tumble
Of the apple,
The gold pelt of the peach
That sometimes falling
Trembles the ground
Like short rain.

And I know the farmer's barn,
Its stacked lofts
Of shining straw
Where I sometimes slide
And coil.
And I know the napping mouse
I will unhinge my jaw
To swallow.

Do not call me.
I do not listen to air.
I listen to the earth
Shiver with every step
Large and small
The whole world takes.

Your heat fills the wind.
The two rivers of my tongue
Fork the air

And I know your scent,
The whole taste of you.

If you would know me,
Then here, take my skin,
The whole husk
Of me.

Kerry Shawn Keys

Song for the Weaver

Weaver, red-haired lover, silver-scaled daughter
of wind and water, weave us a sweetgrass
hammock to make love in, weave the earth
a song to sway in, a fire to dream in.

Make the warp our cries, the weft our laughter,
the evening sun pokeweed and madder,
the morning sun turquoise and soft white angora.
Weaver, weave the moon into the water.

Spin your hair for the fringe and border
with fingers lovely as the falling rain,
weave us a sweetgrass hammock to lie in
in summer's easygoing deepest green.

Then, Weaver, summon your sisters in Autumn,
weave me a hammock of blue dahlias and snow,
weave me a hammock with your heart for a coffin
fastened to the wind and moon in the forest below.

E. G. Burrows

In Late October

My ear may have it wrong,
that half-song heard
faintly by first light among
the farther silences, a phrase
that took months to say
and may be robin
or the creak of a closing door.

The body swarms
with buried incidents, memories
that intersect, dissolve, or become
distinct landscapes, argot lost
with other echoes
and the loneliness of remote tongues.
The tune is fragmentary,

or incomprehensible like mail
months delayed, strewn
over the mat, unanswerable
invitations, blessings out of season
wrongly forwarded or refused,
something that should have flown
but pulled up short.

My ear may know.
We have shared the throwaway,
the wry admission, the aside,
with such transients who cling
to the blood-red berries of firethorn
in late October: robins
who sometimes sing.

Carol Snyder Halberstadt

The Road Is Not a Metaphor

There are no symbols. Only
the hesitant, the shy slight wonder
and bewildered glance
of an animal
crossing the road.

The road is not a metaphor: it cuts
through trees,
the rocks fall away,
even the sea parts, helpless at its coming.
These are signs—intent on passage
through borrowed air
and water, oiled and torn.

The earth bleeds and the cut trees—
these are not metaphors,
they happen inside
the tense and fragile skin
at the very edge.

Eran Williams

Language of Trees

When we learn the language of trees
will we dig our own graves and wait in their depth,
invest in river banks,
make love through wind,
stand naked in weather,
stretch in all directions at once,
keep our first year always on the outside,
drink through straws,
count time through the listings of the earth,
reincarnate as violins and cardboard,
seduce the rain, suck it up, and spit it back at the sky?
When we learn the language of trees
will we hear the seasons pulse,
and find the heart's beat is but an echo?

Barry Sternlieb

The Final Taste

With bow season almost here,
two whitetail does become moonlight
searching for apples. Down near
the burly old tree they browse like

sisters, or mother and daughter. Quietly
I step out on the porch to get
a better look. Frost arches an ivory
back along midnight. My breath,

given body, tells me I'm destined
for the greatness of fallen apples
going bad on the lawn, this second
discovered by sudden muzzles,

crushed and swallowed, the final taste
of earth putting everything in its place.

Hunter's Sabbath—Hippocratic

the gauzy lichen here took years
to mask this granite patient earth
I know I will not save nor cure
invading yet today my path
as often will be hare's and deer's
and cat's described by scat and track
thin trail out thin trail back
that I may leave no greater scar
than they incise on scarp and peak
in easy passing unpursued
nor greater wound than weather makes
in any less than fevered mood
today I will not prey nor storm
my way may do no earthly good
but let it do at least no harm

Suzanne Freeman

Sapillo Creek

Stream-scoured & flood-tumbled
the rocks in a creek-bed
wear down to a smoothness,
like old friends on a backpacking trip
   they've weathered it all.
Waters of a wild mountain
strip stones & souls of rough edges,
revealing shades of twilight & full moon,
the soft colors of acceptance;
captured flecks of quartz & mica
shine back a secret
and the journey was the learning of it.

Jeanne Lohmann

October Moon, New England Church

The full moon's reflected light
blesses the fallen and blazing
sacrament of leaves on the ground,
beech and oak the last to go,
into thin glacial soil where life
lives on granite. The creatures
are preparing, hoarding
what they will need.

Fatten yourself like the moon
and get ready for sleep, then
while the earth freezes around you
move in your house like a tunnel,
stretch your full length of muscle and sinew,
your blood warmer than the snake's
who may not make it.

When you are called to come out into spring
perhaps then will be the time to live,
when hunger has taught you to be thin,
graceful as a spire narrowing into heaven.

If you sleep far enough and long
your eyes returning from the dark
to the waking green of the world
will be luminous with gifts,
each astonishment you thought lost
you take with you, into the sun.

Hermes Almeida Jr.

one dark heart beat

and then in the wet field a chorus of birds
    sixty or seventy of them
        rose

sudden consensus of rising
    angling off in one rippling flag
        underwings

flashing grey in the shimmer upwards, higher
    till the dark bell grows taut
        a heart beat

and wings tilt to shift into another
    angle against the sky, like
        redound of wave,

again to pinnacle and poise and again
    this huge winking page
        arrows

for the grass hopping as they touch
    like windblown leaves
        and are still

Joseph Powell

Early Snow

Outside, the slanting snows, like driven souls.
Up they climb the swirling air
and down they fall, and falling go.
They're blown this way, this way and that.
Love, Love, what can be left to know?
Here's much better than what's there.
This country's roads are filling up with snow.

John Haines

The Ghost Towns

"The North is strewn with cities
of one winter. . . ."

I have seen them, the tinderboxes
stacked upon each other,
their wind-structures fallen,
no way to enter now but the gates of frost.

They were lighted by the pressure
lamps of fever, by lamp-men
trimming soot and breaking coal,
reading by the fire of their wicks
the cold logic of the snow.

It was all dream and delirium,
the amazed rumor of gold—a letter
carried in a stampeder's pocket,
unread, and the homeland long forgotten.

As I have held my hand above a candle,
seen the red flesh glow
and the knotted bones darken,

so will these buildings leave
their trusses charred and crossed,
the graveyards lettered
with a script no one can read. . . .

And over the bleak and gutted land
no wall to stop the wind—
one space, one frame for all.

Paul Willis

San Rafael Mountain

It takes a while for the country to settle
into our eyes. A weekend,
a lifetime, is not enough. The ridges
rise from the distant wall of the blue Sierra
to the beaten folds of the Santa Ynez.
On the horizon, last and lost,
Santa Cruz and the sun-bright islands.
River of ocean wheels the prow
of Point Conception to Morro Bay
and the first dark jut of the Big Sur coast.
We see all these from the mountaintop
in a moment of time. But we cannot lay
claim to these kingdoms. As much as we ache
to join our souls to the slopes of grace
we must wait for them. We must wait
for the land. We must wait for the condor
who spirals again in the winter sun
above Sisquoc, above Hurricane Deck, above San Rafael,
who sees the earth spread out below
as it has not been seen for years, who sees us here
no bigger than bespectacled mice, peering
through our tinted glass until we know
as we are known.

Mary Oliver

Lonely, White Fields

Every night
  the owl
    with his wild monkey-face
      calls through the black branches

and the mice freeze
  and the rabbits shiver
    in the snowy fields—
      and then there is the long, deep trough of silence

when he stops singing, and steps
  into the air.
    I don't know
      what death's ultimate

purpose is, but I think
  this: whoever dreams of holding his
    life in his fist
      year after year into the hundreds of years

has never considered the owl—
  how he comes, exhausted,
    through the snow,
      through the icy trees,

past snags and vines, wheeling
out of barns and church steeples,
turning this way and that way
through the mesh of every obstacle—

undeterred by anything—
filling himself time and time again
with a red and digestible joy
sickled up from the lonely, white fields—

and how at daybreak,
as though everything had been done
that must be done, the fields
swell with a rosy light,

the owl fades
back into the black branches,
the snow goes on falling
flake after perfect flake.

Five

Distance and Depth

Whether looking down through
a pond's surface, past a mossy
tavern of twigs into a floating nest
and through the membrane of a single
translucent egg globule floating there,
down into the drama and complex
carnival of the jelly mote, its lipids
and ashes and crystal inclusions,
through its loops and plots
and domestications, past its gates
and messages, its storms, signs,
and orbits, on down towards
the tense purple nebula of chaos
at its core;

or whether watching far out, over
the flat grasses and gulleys, skimming
the plains, past low opuntia, hidden
beeflies, jumping mice, the burrows
of dogs and deer and all that multitude,
right up to the first rising red rock
range and past that to the next sheer
evergreen plateau and on beyond
to the ultimate highest blue snow
of the peaks with names, past them
to the ragged ridge of the sinking moon
and behind that into the easy black

where the eyes seem suddenly turned
hard and fast on themselves;

whether in distance or in depth,
either way it's evident there are fields
and fields and fields aplenty, more
space than is needed, ample space
for any kind of sin to be laid down,
disassembled, swallowed away,
consumed, forgotten, lost,
if one should only ask
for such a favor.

Marijane Osborn

Gift

We walk by the river and
brooding he talks
first of the insubstantial world
then of the *torus*, of smoke, of particles
of ice like Saturn's rings, he's catching
fire now, of galaxies, of endless light,
tori turning but flowing also
outside to in and inward out again,
always flowing, always the same,
moods, souls, rivers, trees. . . .

"What are you doing?" I ask.
Bending, he removes rock by
riversmooth rock, revealing
a perfect discarded snakeskin, frozen
like a photograph of smoke or
particles of ice, a breath of coil,
its empty eyespace gleaming
of elsewhere as I hold it to the sun.

Charlie Mehrhoff

Before the Frost

Wrapped myself
in the skin
of the earth,
in the souls
of pine needles
longing for the sun.
Stones grew
from my eye sockets.
Ants carried away
the flesh
of my face.
Mule deer feasted
upon the fruit
of my breasts.
Swallows dove
through my ribs,
there
to taste the sweetness
of the dark soil.

It took years
for the moonlight
to fade the walls
of my skull.
Years
before I was able

to breathe.
Years
before I was able
to find my way
home.

David Wagoner

Gray Fox in a Roadside Zoo

Around and across his pen, light-footed, the fox
At every turn brushes the dark brush
Of his tail against wire-mesh, wearing deep grooves
In the ground among weeds like paths crosshatching snow,
Ears pricked, tail floating now, returning
To where he was and will be, his muzzle lifted
To the fields and woods he remembers perfectly
Over the road (where he knew at any moment
Of day how he should sleep
Or by night where to wait or stalk or run on the hunt
Or go to earth), his precise paws scarcely touching,
And curving so evenly in a level balance
He is almost weightless on the trace of nothing.

Blackbirds

For two weeks now their wheezing treetop patter
has been a kind of daytime serenade,
music lacking melody and matter.
Their whistling and clucking, those notes played
by hinges gone ungreased so long they squeal
when forced ajar, are anything but song.
They're up there by the hundreds. What appeal
bids them congregate? Is their need to throng
so great that blathering is no disgrace
and the solitary voice should have no say?
It's doubtful conversation's taking place.
But something does get said. Every day
near dusk, with one mind their black clouds rise,
leaving silence empty as their yellow eyes.

Whitetails

The husks of yellow berries move
like soundless bells
as their bodies brush against them.
Their scents cling to them like loose
clothing as they cross the road
and slip in among the bare limbs
and dry grass. The snow, old snow,
crunches and creaks beneath them,
and the dense air, cold and still,
holds the sound of their steps
and their breathing. They move
in a line through the trees above
the stream, shadowing the stream's course.
A breath or sigh, some human sound stops
in the air. White tails go up
in warning. The buck glides up
through the trees a few yards
and stops. Three does. Four.
The buck fixes his eyes on a point
above the snow, ears and tail erect,
body poised. I stand still
returning his stare. He moves
his long muscled neck with a quick
birdlike motion once, twice
to fasten his eyes more securely

upon me. And for a moment
we define each other's world
joined at eye level and heartbeats
above the snow.

Diane Morgan

The Cave

The dripping fingers point and press inexorably to earth.
To clay. At forty-five degrees below the heat
Of human blood, they pulse precarious
Within the blackened veins of earth.
A hundred years and more it takes
To drip one calcite inch.
And inch by calcite inch
They flow to stone
And pierce their
Limestone
Vault.

Within that crystalled capsuled
Darkness
The gypsy gray bat squeaks
And swirls its dervish wings.
Living calcite, a quick bat of a cave's eye,
It will, at last, wings shut, eyes shut,
Heart and blood shut down,
Hang upside down
And point to earth.

Leonard Nathan

The Naturalist

Nature led him blindly
through its fabulous shadows
down a stony path
paved by a dead glacier.

Suddenly old, he finds
himself staring blindly
through his worried students
and listening far away.

There's nothing out there really—
scree and a windy silence,
not even a bird
to call it, singing, home.

W. S. Merwin

Late

The old walls half fallen sink away under brambles
    and ivy and trail off into the oak woods that have been coming
back for them through all the lives whose daylight
    has vanished into the mosses there was a life once
in which I lived here part of a life believing
    in it partly as though it were the whole story
and so not a story at all and partly knowing
    that I clung to it only in passing as in
the blink of an eye and that partly I was where
    I had come from and now when I come back long afterwards
and find it still here I remember it as a story
    I know but no longer believe and that is my place in it

Carol Snyder Halberstadt

What Is There

There are these books
and the bright red berries
drying slowly on a tree,
seen through the glass
of the library windows,
and the bridge to there
is only to make visible
what cannot be seen—
no art can do this.

We breathe,
counting,
and measuring what is there—
it is all around us,
wandering,
we walk inside it
on dark paths of December's mud.

It is only the body that fails.
The light in the reeds is there
and the dried grasses,
their stalks brittle in the cold air,
their seeds shed,
season after season.

Greg Glazner

Fishing: The Late Wish

Thigh-deep in heavy waders,
he'd waited hours for the water
to reveal a winter brown. No motion
in the pools, no current-flash

or thrashing, but a few enormous flakes
were falling. He half-believed the crows,
whose calls were muffled, lovely
above the drifted hills, might swirl down

with the snow, and dissolve
into that frigid, empty rolling.
And as ice began to pearl
the eyelets of his rod, and the lure,

for hours, fell unbidden
to each swell and freezing stillness,
he understood how a living fisherman
could long to lie back there

and let the river drift him
past all knowing, so the vault of days
could glaze away his face's hollows,
encrust the risen tips of his boots,

and float the polished emblem of a body
fusing with ice floes, shrouded whiter
in each snow, silent to the marrow
with the perfection of the January cold.

David Axelrod

Tithe

Some apples always remain
just out of reach of three-legged
ladders and our outstretched hands.

By October, yellow jackets
growl inside overripe fruit
that never falls, no matter the wind:

russet globes hang high in the trees,
rusting, mushy, molding,
but sweet inside,

a drunken feast for those of us
who haven't forgotten our great
wings, and how we can fly.

It isn't really a generous thing
to concede a tenth part,
though it's no less our boon

when—in the crowns of those trees,
in January, the sky low and bleak—
nuthatch, waxwing, towhee,

and the loud, misanthropic jay,
hungry vagrants of the snow,
jabber as though at their Jubilee.

Paulann Petersen

Pragmatics

In your story of bees,
they slowly fill an outside wall—
three stud-spaces wide, two storeys high—
in the front bay of your old farmhouse.
You first try all the poisons,

even your pickup set
to run all day, its exhaust
piped into a hole in the wall—
while you go away, hoping the fumes
will kill them. But no.

So on a winter's icy morning
you pull the siding off
and scrape out, storey by tall storey,
thick clots of comb and honey,
clumps of stiff, chilled bees.

They had to go. No question.
But tell me again, please,
how you stood inside and breathed—
in summer's reckless heat—
the fragrance of their work,

wild perfume of wax and flower.
Say again how you pressed your ear
tight to the wall, heard the house humming,
felt its blur of countless wings,
a fine, even tremble.

What Loss Is

What is it we are saying
about ourselves when we fail
so many? I dream

often that the wolves weave
down to us
off the hills, and it's as if,
like a print, love is made over
and over in me. Saving

myself means keeping them
moving like fire
among the trees, breathing
me back into something
resembling my life. How much
I love this earth is answered

here, where the wolves run
all day, sometimes
all night, oiled and blazing
with their own hunger. They pass

like love
across something less
and more than distance, something

I might step out on and so walk
and walk and not come back.

Al Ortolani

Hunting New Cave on Cecil Creek

Along the road that leads to Cecil Creek,
the black-limbed fingers of maples, oaks and elms
stretch maplike into the stoney silence.

If a man follows them, then he follows himself
to where a blackbird flies the dome of winter sky,
the rush of wind through wing feathers

as hushed as limestone,
gray, solid as the quiet within.

Maryann Whalen

Winter: Woman Looking from the Window at a Spruce Tree

The sunlight catches in the heart
as if to stir a deeper self to memory
of a time gone, another life of
knowing the self as sunlight.
Not a small shy animal,
not a mystic saint or an
uncounted peasant hoeing corn,
but sunlight, playing alone in winter,
along a branch, moving lightly,
settling lightly on crystallized snow
held gently there, not especially warm,
but light, being right and not thinking.
The earth was younger then,
in the deep green shine of spruce.

Though not still, self was silent then
and is that now, ineffably held.

Mary Oliver

Winter

And the waves
gush pearls
from their snowy throats
as they come
leaping
over the moss-green,
black-green,
glass-green roughage—
as they crumble
on the incline
scattering
whatever they carry
in their invisible
and motherly
hands:
stones,
sea weed,
mussels
icy and plump,
with waled shells,
waiting
for the gatherers
who come flying
on their long white wings—
who comes walking,
who comes muttering:
thank you,

old dainties,
dark wreckage,
coins of the sea
in my pockets,
and plenty for the gulls,
and the wind still pounding
and the sea still streaming in like a mother wild with gifts—
in this world I am as rich
as I need to be.

Acknowledgments

Hermes Almeida Jr., "one dark heart beat." © 1993 by Hermes Almeida Jr. Reprinted by permission of the poet.

T. K. André-Eames, "Under the Sun." © 1991 by T. K. André-Eames. Reprinted by permission of the poet.

Antler, "A Second Before It Bursts." © 1993 by Antler. Reprinted by permission of the poet.

David Axelrod, "Tithe." © 1998 by David Axelrod.

Bruce Berger, "Visitation." © 1989 by Bruce Berger. Reprinted by permission of the poet.

Wendell Berry, "The Vacation." From *Entries* by Wendell Berry (Pantheon Books, 1994). © 1994 by Wendell Berry. Reprinted by permission. "The Best Reward" and "The Lowland Grove" from *The Collected Sabbath Poems* by Wendell Berry (Counterpoint, 1998). © 1998 by Wendell Berry. Reprinted by permission of the poet and Counterpoint.

Robert Bly, "A Private Fall." © 1994 by Robert Bly. Reprinted by permission of the poet.

E. G. Burrows, "In Late October." © 1989 by Edwin Gladding Burrows. Reprinted by permission of the poet.

Don Colburn, "Morning Song." © 1998 by Don Colburn.

John Daniel, "Spring Burning." © 1996 by John Daniel. First appeared in the *Texas Observer.*

Alison Hawthorne Deming, "Sanctuary." From *The Monarchs: A Poem Sequence* by Alison Hawthorne Deming (Louisiana State University Press, 1997). © 1997 by Alison Hawthorne Deming. Reprinted by permission.

John Daniel is the author of two poetry collections, *Common Ground* and *All Things Touched by Wind*; a book of nature essays, *The Trail Home*; and a memoir, *Looking After*. He lives in western Oregon.

Alison Hawthorne Deming's *Science and Other Poems* won the 1993 Walt Whitman Award. *The Monarchs: A Poem Sequence* is her most recent book. She directs the University of Arizona Poetry Center.

Letha Elliott is an actor and singer as well as a writer. She currently works in nonprofit arts administration for the Memphis Arts Council.

Suzanne Freeman lives in Austin, Texas.

Reginald Gibbons's latest books are *Sparrow: New and Selected Poems* (Louisiana State University Press) and *Sweetbitter*, a novel (Penguin, 1996). He was editor of *TriQuarterly* from 1981 to 1997.

Jody Gladding lives in East Calais, Vermont. Her book, *Stone Crop*, appeared in the Yale Younger Poets Series in 1993.

Malcolm Glass directs the writing program at Austin Peay State University. A recent Fulbrighter in Slovenia, he has published four books of poetry and five books on writing.

Greg Glazner's books of poetry are *From the Iron Chair* and *Singularity*, both published by W. W. Norton. He is coeditor of *Countermeasures* magazine.

Mary Gray's stories and poems have appeared in numerous magazines and journals. Her first novel, *When a Bird Dreams*, is currently being edited for publication.

John Haines's most recent book is *At the End of This Summer: Poems 1948–54*, Copper Canyon Press, 1997. A collection of essays, *Fables and Distances*, was published by Graywolf Press in 1996. He lives in Anchorage.

Carol Snyder Halberstadt is an artist, an art teacher, and an editor as well as a poet. She publishes poetry and deals in Native American art on her website, www.migrations.com. She lives near Boston.

Contributors

Hermes Almeida Jr. is a singer and songwriter living in Seattle. "one dark heart beat" is his first published poem.

T. K. André-Eames's work has appeared in magazines such as *Louisiana Literature*, the *Southern Review*, and a text published by the Indian Council of Education. She teaches in Baton Rouge, Louisiana.

Antler, author of *Factory* (City Lights) and *Last Words* (Ballantine), has poems in more than eighty anthologies, including *Earth Prayers, Erotic by Nature*, and *American Poets Say Goodbye to the 20th Century*.

David Axelrod is the author of two books of poetry, *Jerusalem of Grass* and *The Kingdom at Hand*. His work appears in many literary journals. He lives with his family in eastern Oregon.

Bruce Berger's poetry collection *Facing the Music* appeared from Confluence Press, 1995. His collection of desert essays, *The Telling Distance*, won the 1990 Western States Book Award.

Wendell Berry, of Henry County, Kentucky, is the author most recently of *Entries* (poems), *Another Turn of the Crank* (essays), and *A World Lost*, a novel. *The Collected Sabbath Poems* will be published by Counterpoint in 1998.

Robert Bly's latest books are *The Sibling Society*, on the failure of adulthood in the United States; *The Soul Is Here for Its Own Joy*, a collection of sacred poems from many languages; and *Morning Poems*, a collection of new poems.

E. G. Burrows's poetry collections include *The Arctic Tern, Man Fishing, Kiva, The House of August*, and several chapbooks. "In Late October" was reprinted in *The Birds Under the Earth*, Owl Creek Press, 1997.

Don Colburn, a reporter at the *Washington Post*, has an MFA from Warren Wilson College. He won the Discovery/*The Nation* Award for poetry in 1993.

Marc Harshman has written nine picture books for children, including *The Storm* (Cobblehill/Dutton), a Smithsonian Notable Book for Children. He lives in Marshall County, West Virginia.

Jane Hirshfield, author of *The Lives of the Heart* and *The October Palace* (both HarperCollins), has received a Guggenheim Fellowship, the Poetry Center Book Award, and many other honors. She lives in the San Francisco Bay area.

Laney Iglehart is a writer and hiker who lives near the Gunpowder River in the quietly beautiful countryside of Glencoe, Maryland.

William Johnson lives with his wife and family in Lewiston, Idaho. He has written a critical study, *What Thoreau Said* (University of Idaho, 1990), and a chapbook of poems, *At the Wilderness Boundary* (Confluence, 1996).

Roger Jones has published one book, *Strata*, and presently teaches at Southwest Texas State University.

Russell Kesler teaches at the University of Central Florida, where he is editor of the *Florida Review*.

Kerry Shawn Keys is publisher of Pine Press, soon to relocate to the Czech Republic. He is a translator from the Brazilian Portuguese and the author of more than fifteen books of poetry, including *A Gathering of Smoke* and *Decay's Desire*.

Maxine Kumin won the Pulitzer Prize for *Up Country* in 1973. Her *Selected Poems 1960–1990* has just been published by Norton.

Sydney Lea is the author of six poetry collections, most recently, *To the Bone*; a novel, *A Place in Mind*; and a collection of naturalist essays, *Hunting the Whole Way Home*.

Stephen Lefebure's poetry has appeared in *Birmingham Poetry Review*, *Kansas Quarterly*, *Literary Review*, *Plains Poetry Journal*, and *Weber Studies*.

Denise Levertov lives in Seattle. One of her most recent books is a selection of her poems on nature, *The Life Around Us* (New Directions, 1997).

Jeanne Lohmann lives in Olympia, Washington. Her collections include *Between Silence and Answer* (Pendle Hill, 1994) and *Granite Under Water* (Fithian, 1996). She is poetry editor for *Earthlight* magazine.

Arthur McLean lives in Mobile, Alabama.

Charlie Mehrhoff writes under the pseudonym Scarecrow. His poetry appears in *Lightning & Ash* and *Nexus,* occasionally *The Sun.* He lives in northern New Mexico.

W. S. Merwin's most recent book is *Lament for the Makers* (Counterpoint, 1996). He lives near Haiku, Hawaii.

Carolyn Miller is a writer and freelance book editor living in San Francisco. Her poems have appeared in the *Georgia Review, ZYZZYVA, Quarterly West,* and *Shenandoah.*

Deborah A. Miranda is an enrolled member of the Esselen Nation, a California tribe. Her *Indian Cartography* won the 1997 Diane Decorah Memorial First Book Award and will be published in 1998 by the Greenfield Review Press.

Diane Morgan lives in Williamsport, Maryland.

Leonard Nathan's latest book, *The Diary of a Left-handed Bird Watcher* (Graywolf, 1996), is a prose meditation on bird watching. He is better known as a poet and the author of *Carrying On: New and Selected Poems.*

John Nixon Jr. has spent most of his life in Mississippi and Virginia. A former editor of *The Lyric,* he has contributed to numerous magazines, newspapers, and anthologies.

Jude Nutter, born in Yorkshire, England, holds masters degrees in women's studies and creative writing. She teaches at the University of Oregon and is studying to be a paramedic.

Naomi Shihab Nye's recent books are *Habibi,* a novel for young readers, *Lullaby Raft, Never in a Hurry* (essays), and *Fuel* (poems). She lives in San Antonio, Texas.

Mary Oliver has received both the Pulitzer Prize and the National Book Award for her poetry. She is also the author of a book of essays and a handbook on poetry. She lives in Vermont and teaches at Bennington College.

Al Ortolani, a hiker, caver, and kayaker, teaches high school and college English in Pittsburg, Kansas. His poetry has appeared in *The Quarterly*, the *English Journal*, the *Midwest Quarterly*, and other magazines.

Marijane Osborn has lived and taught in several countries—three times as a Fulbright Lecturer in Iceland—and is current chair of medieval studies at the University of California, Davis.

Greg Pape lives with his family in the Bitterroot Valley and teaches in the writing program at the University of Montana. His most recent books include *Storm Pattern* (University of Pittsburgh, 1992) and *Sunflower Facing the Sun* (University of Iowa, 1992).

Paulann Petersen's poems have appeared in *Poetry* and the *New Republic*, and are now on the Tri-Met buses in Portland, Oregon, as part of the Poetry in Motion Project.

Joseph Powell teaches English at Central Washington University. His third book, *Getting There*, was recently published by the *Quarterly Review of Literature*.

John Quinn's poems, stories, and articles have appeared in many academic journals and general interest magazines. His books are *The Wolf Last Seen* and *Easy Pie*. He lives and teaches in Cedar Falls, Iowa.

C. L. Rawlins was born, and lives a rather windblown life, in the state of Wyoming. His poems appear in *Ploughshares*, *Quarterly West*, *Poetry Wales*, and *Poetry Ireland Review*, and his prose wanders all over the map.

Andrés Rodríguez is the author of a study of Keats, *Book of the Heart* (Lindisfarne Press, 1993), and a collection of poems, *Night Song* (Tia Chucha Press, 1994). He lives in Kansas City.

Pattiann Rogers's *Firekeeper: New and Selected Poems* appeared in 1994 from Milkweed Editions. *Eating Bread and Honey* was published in 1997 by the same press. She lives in Colorado.

Reg Saner's *Reaching Keet Seel: Our Present Past and the Anasazi* is due out from the University of Utah Press in 1998. Three of his poetry collections have won national awards.

Tom Sexton is Alaska's Poet Laureate. His latest book is *A Blossom of Snow* (Mad River Press).

Thomas R. Smith's most recent book of poems is *Horse of Earth* (Holy Cow! Press, 1994). He lives in western Wisconsin.

Ronald F. Smits teaches English at Indiana University of Pennsylvania and lives in Ford City, Pennsylvania. His poems have appeared most recently in *Poetry East*, *Radical Teacher*, and the *Southern Review*.

William Stafford was born in Hutchinson, Kansas, in 1914, and died in Lake Oswego, Oregon, in 1993. His selected poems will be published by Graywolf Press in 1998.

Barry Sternlieb, publisher of Mad River Press in Richmond, Massachusetts, is the author of *Thoreau's Hat* and *Thinning the Rows*, both from Brooding Heron Press.

Jonathan Till, an archaeologist, lives in Bluff, Utah. He is constantly awed by the Colorado Plateau's broad span of human history from PaleoIndian mammoth hunters to Mormon uranium miners.

Eric Trethewey's latest book is *The Long Road Home*. He is a professor of English at Hollins College and lives in Catawba, Virginia.

David Wagoner has published fifteen books of poems, most recently *Walt Whitman Bathing* (University of Illinois, 1996), and ten novels. He edits *Poetry Northwest*.

Ronald Wallace's ten books include *The Uses of Adversity*, *Time's Fancy*, and *The Makings of Happiness*, all from the University of Pittsburgh Press. He directs the creative writing program at the University of Wisconsin, Madison.

Ingrid Wendt, of Eugene, Oregon, has authored two books of poems and is coeditor of the Oregon poetry anthology *From Here We Speak*. "The Thing to Do" remembers the D. H. Lawrence Ranch in Taos, New Mexico.

Maryann Whalen, a reading specialist, is a southerner now living in Nova Scotia. Her most recent work has appeared in *Nashwaak Review* and *Antigonish Review*.

Eran Williams, a native of Santa Cruz, currently teaches at San Jose State University. His poetry has appeared in *Exquisite Corpse*, *ONTHEBUS*, *Reed*, and other magazines. He is writing a novel.

Paul Willis is an associate professor of English at Westmont College in Santa Barbara, California. His work appeared in *Best American Poetry 1996* (Scribner).

Kathryn Winograd has published poems in many journals, including the *Denver Quarterly*, *The Journal*, and *TriQuarterly*.

DATE

Printed in the United States
114283LV00001B/25/A